Certain Fathoms

Certain Fathoms

Bonny Cassidy

PUNCHER & WATTMANN

First published in 2012
Published by Puncher and Wattmann
PO Box 441
Glebe NSW 2037

http://www.puncherandwattmann.com

puncherandwattmann@bigpond.com

National Library of Australia
Cataloguing-in-Publication entry:

Cassidy, Bonny

Certain Fathoms

ISBN   9781921450372

I. Title.

A821.3

Cover design by Matthew Holt

Printed by McPhersons Printing Group

This project has been assisted by the Australian Government through the Australia Council, its arts funding and advisory body.

Australian Government

Australia Council
for the Arts

Contents

Certain fathoms

... the ring on the finger becomes thin beneath by wearing, the fall of
dripping water hollows the stone, the bent iron ploughshare secretly grows
smaller in the fields, and we see the paved stone streets worn away by the feet
of the multitude; again, by the city-gates the brazen statues reveal that their
right hands are wearing thin...

Lucretius, *De Rerum Natura*

The long world

Serrata

The hour, I can't tell.
Not yet blueing: but open and clean cut,
when matter twists
     by algebra
        or freak
then turns again.
Breathe grip, breathing gripping under dark, serrata
        shadows the fleshcoloured wall
trunks 200 per cent, leaves the size of nebulae,
       (sprayed black), the scale so close
to the eye they might be motes.   So close I doubt myself

squared in the bathroom window, telling.

Figure

after the botanical drawings of Margaret Stones

And winter, a swarm of hard flat spores.

Pressed and packed into myself
I followed them
under a field
light as shale, its wild melons striped with fuchsia bush.

Across the terrace, now: figs waving
great tides of approval
their nodding planes.
On good thick pages I begin
my coloured science.

A peace between,
where woolly head fixes its barbs
against a pencil flourish
even as it spins
deep into the paper's grain.

There's more remembering
than beauty—those humming seconds of sight:
testing the spike
'til it feathers brittle on my thumbtip
mixing a slipper of pink
to fill a petal

leaving the blank halo of scale
that I long to complicate.

Bubbles grow over the stem,
one lifting away rolling up
toward the stamens
clear beckonings coming loose and dark.

First a thickness then
a happy signature.

                    I thought to go without—

                    spreading shade by inches
                    and drawing green minutes of sustenance.
                    They lasted:
                            I discovered them—all vein
                    still growing between the blotting sheets and blocks.

                    I earthed rough drafts
                    brought from the mouth
                    of the pen, line lengthening
                    a flower's hour or flushing a turn of death.
                    Tough yellow parchment I kept for best.

Wind is scuttling
a few seeds from a jarred bloom.
I shield them off the table

a crush of pollen under heel.

This examined art. The way
soft tissue's brought to measure
before it browns and spooks itself.
One piece.

Over a thin red indent
curve shoulders—
under it, legs folded in creases.
My face, the lamp.

Gould's Resplendent Trogon

There is that
     great reach of paper before bird

     rolled out like a score
          minus noise

          A square sky followed
          by the drop of the resplendent trogon—
          in multiple exposure
          its resplendence—
               languishing: longhand
               of tail scooped to the frame.

After the burial

His right foot drags a distracted waltz
as if the way back lingers behind—
to a time of still
before he were wiser—
a time that comes after
this, after.
His legs snap shut. And only
these hired mules fill the cone of dust
before the next heave forward.
As they bungle right through it on the double,
he imagines animals alone
must own that ringing time,
always between one step and another.

En abyme (Northland)

for Tim

Talk is breaking, breaking. In these minutes you
and I seem to be history without lineage.
But something made us
and so it lies in our pit
like a seam turned in.

      We cross the flats that sign the Narrows.

      A thumbnail church is lodged
      under the cloud-marsh. As we hover past,
      kauri bellow in the harbour.

Our conversation is a twister of dust, swarming points:
that courtship of matter—
the touch and the go.

      Our car points at a dune
      caped in ozone, sponging
      off joints of whale. We empty their fluted trunks.
      "Birds and fishes visit us and disappear."

There is no line to draw from there to here.
There's a cone of thinning and thickening souvenirs. I am
when we speak, and this time we speak
of vultures: how they die, not by falling but rising
to splinter softly—sky ribbon
somewhere up, beyond belief—prey plaited into their atoms,
or dropping a fraction into the path
of their own, to be shared between
earth and everything else.

> A tui swings itself
> against the cliff and grips
>
> as we cast pebbles
> against slipped onyx—
> a wall of sound fixing back the tide, its stinging grains
> pass over
>
> dusk and a cobalt eel waiting in the creek.

Before you leave again I hear you say, just once,
perhaps the vulture eats itself
and your words in delay finally settle into me, then you—
years away and oceans parting.

POV

Those geraniums she planted
beginning to enter the square: softly, a series
of green blinks. They barely move through
the closing atmosphere.
She touches the stump
at the garden's centre;
no one goes there

only white swells of cloud and her green eyes.
Good things come.

Ab ovo

Flush with jet. The lantern lands.
        As clouds unpeel, swollen leans—
        a small applause from within. Minor eclipse.

                            I lift a vase and watch
                            the pods kick

                            rolling sage plans.

        I catch them just
        as they bounce out
        onto their knees.
                A little figure flees
            forward   to pat the shining
        bellow, lest it draw breath. Still, structure uplifts and bothers
                at the silk now close to red.

                    What ease   magpies weave the web of ropes.

                  Its last huff flies out
                  carelessly, like genius.

                  Its strings disappear into floor.

                  Circles concentrating upon one another.

Untitlement

Surely you remember how sunlight came
under that gap and around, leaking
into the vacated room to drop
behind the door, where you'd left a robe
and then flew up to the cornice, but more

dimly,
                              surely.

Vector

a)

The kid's hand

wheeling
I turn the sting, it's wrist

b)

its way
to my hand, a right moth turn:
      the kid's sting.

Crying my hand, springing back
      my wheel

c)

turning the kid's hand

it enters mine, sprung around the wrist.
      Kid in hand   K's away

moth to the right
kid turns, enters

my head that its wrist

saying, mother, pointing

Escort

When the flat came
        into view
he heard so many words, they fell from the windows
into clumps of garden.

He could see straight through the stairwell

positioned so its cavities met.

Its arrow-slits where cacti grew sturdy lobes.
All the words flooding
down the pencil pine.

Hand to mouth

... verse is a wide net
Through which many subtleties escape.
Nor would I take it to capture a strong thing,
Such as a whale.
(Anna Wickham, 'Note on Rhyme')

It's almost impossible. I stand here being mumbled,
hearing the bay's mouth from above (water dull as traffic),
sight bigger than tongue.
        Here, in crests of hanging sand, pipers fidget—
their sunken heads breathe, sift the unjust ratio
earth:sky.

My own mouth contracts at the root. Close enough
to leaching grapes and rolling trash, still my grimace
floods the high tide with simple blocks of space or tonal shifts.
I touch my lip.
        Divers are pushing their skin under the surface,
becoming faded clouds of colour, waving strips, then whole again.
The bay cleans them like bones, takes them in.
It has no hide, but finds light amongst the deep, and wears it.

Women of Venice, Giacometti

Hell chill young widows in the heel of night
(John Berryman, 'Venice, 182–')

Coldly, hangs
the parade
of pegs, palings
or women
weighted. Light
only chucks
their forms
beyond them:
prodigious children.

But the glaring
corner of each—
their muchness
at a certain angle—
the hook and scrawl
of their bodies
an epitaph
to every thing
that has ever
furled into
and out of

Magma

At almost noon.

He sees only figures   no game.

They clap. Céline has the ball.
He raises his palms, then lowers them.

Just go, just go. Clap, laugh, go.

Their shadows curl
under them: falling leaves.
The ball hovers above the beach, in front of the sun.
He eases back

he becomes sand.

Obit (Unmoved)

Lick your lips. Uneven road.
You eat passing images
through the car window

the more you look   you missed—
those streaky plains, *people as big as football fields*—
that was real, this is then.

You barely chew; the past is frozen into distance.
The radio jumps

and lands on an obit:
the Snakeman of Florida, dead at 100:
his daily venom
his numb, stunned health.

And jumps. The heat off sound.

Cramming and cooling of the eye. Invincible

you knock at the glass, know at once
how he grew old—flicking fear, hearing events approach like tides.

Alarmist

I wait between tile and rug.
The clock's a cake.

You and your chest hang—their folds
and the rest suspended beneath. Shut.

Unheard, lunch on the terrace slowly eating itself.

You miss twigs, the grinding Whirlpool.
Minutes tip, empty of breath.

Static expands into the room.
I hear legs shifting beneath you.

Welcome

Gold pours from the hospital roof, spelling
Welcome. A neon cross turns

above the old nativity—
its wet lamb propped on a step,
purple turbans like planets.

Inside, the empty aviary.

The cousin

She collects plates from the table,
gravy running between them
    soaks into a small spot on her chest.

    Old wine once spilt onto the kitchen stones.
        This was a girls' home, once, you told her

        girls' stones.

The child pulls herself up the hill
        to the heat of birds, a lizard

        the distance barks.

        You are leaning on her memory.

She watches you bang pans together,
and makes from the colander
a hat of a thousand eyes.

    In the garden she can hear the tap running,
    a rush somewhere under the lawn.
        She is standing on it.

        The child holds her arm behind her back
        and walks with a twist of pain, pretending

Don't be silly

After dinner she picks up the plates.

The sauce will need soaking out—
she's packed her spare uniform.

> Once the bath is run
> you phone the mother,
> hear her on a balcony, a car rushing below

> *It'll be weeks*

> Behind you, splashing, her child

> Barks in the distance.

Passenger

I see you, deflating
on blue Illawarra nights—

those empty, practical beaches
that strung so many fits and silences
their length.

From a car sliding up
the black cool of mountain bungalows,

see the city put to rest, behind:
rooms pitched from point to point
of the town. Their large glass sliders
                will be hammered by others' debts or butts.

Rising, a map of islands
that we squinted at in autumn,
folding neatly out from the stacks.

In spring the smoke smudged minor particulars
of land and sea—a new mass to exhale—

because there is that transience, here—
the trains of phrase and acquaintance,
unstopped chains
of heat, return.

Points

I was burnt orange, I'm black.

      As it rises I clarify.

You think I have a front.

      Distantly, as it falls
I have grapes of high-held ash.
My soot is whet.

      If you approach,

      your own personal
                rain.

Romanesque

In a room where a church
has been uprooted, docked and steadied
to the pace of display, he's sure of art:
its vigil of columns and capitals

uncertain a stone was ever scored
for a god alone, or for a saint
set down in the sculptor's brief.
(Was it written, then, in a contract
one bulbous reptile curving from a human head
or told with fulsome gestures as the idea rolled forward?)

There's a concession, he agrees—
a long, smooth core within each work of rock
a hard pearl waning back into its shell—
to make an object of love: a botany
of what's planted in this cloister,
or for the children's chapel, a bird wrapped in fat leaves.

But at his feet there's something
unaccounted for by the steady hand of commerce—
ravenous, it feeds upon itself. Arabesque, and growing.

He follows trunks of limestone horned outwards,
a web-winged dog rolling a hollowed pupil,
the knees of a man that jump to meet his painted mask.
Putting a hand to the white relief,
he senses the artist's reach—
a buzzing drip of water and paint—
as though watching from outside
a lit room.

Guest

Often I'd thought of a boarding house
croaking by sea—
someplace suddenly deep, with a swell-threshed pier
and tidal population. I wasn't the first:

you gaze out from canvas
into wedges of noon; as it angles
you watch legs grow stilts and hear
the loose downpipe shaking
against its balustrade,
wake to the landing wave.

The waiting shape

The underwater streams away,
the wall's cracked at once. A forest

of silhouettes and their conspirators
fade into action——unstuck

hats, crests, the waiting shape.
And strands of grille: cables descending

or rising,
tubes,

bell-pull.
The table drifts.

most of what happens to it
is beyond its control
in the black water beneath its legs

J S Harry, 'standing in front of a woman artist's portrait of a pelican'

Certain fathoms

The rushes

Once I called it the long world

    ignoring a flat one sprung from air

        where the rushes
        freeze their strokes
        and duck shit bobs
        like thought—
       the only tarnish
            that says, wait—

    clamped and staring
    at the bird wedged
in the dark

    white without roots
    or jetty stumps.

      Cloud buckles to weed.

Range

1.

A bird breaks
itself down, ties
its tune into a knot.

Always begin with a bird, like ruling a line
that stretches into angles

an envelope shrieking
its opening
and its closing.

Thus begun, draw in—
so near, the soft-burring edges of green or brown
will frettle under an easterly; so they will,
as a bird, fold over head
slide through marsh lines
pulling both ways into a long unmoving spoon.

2.

A bird calls, spans, slicks up.
Before the air, it was hidden
on a rustling explosion of leaves.

Before the bird, the tree was downriver
somewhere, stalking. Needle falls gave it away.

But don't listen for walking saplings: it's when their droppling
becomes a memory not too distant that it's heard,
and all their scattered picks and knots harden into recognition.

Only the wasps
jammed between rock and earth
are somehow
a chill clean pocket
of ready thoughts,

known at once—

step where the light comes again

quick.

3.
Night's shadow settles in the carpet of the range, even
as noon grows tight. The place is splitting:
high up out of the riverbed
take a different route through its walls.

There's a slip
incised into the bank—a deep shelf
wedged well with kindle and roll, some of it bunched up
to roots, some flipped—

under the rim of earth and wrack
a slip cut round the sandstone skirting: no rushing cavern
(that bird was landing in a puddle after all)
just a deeper crevice   swallowing striped chips of shale.
An opening for some kind of

except it ducks in from the bank
and turns a few metres down
back to the bed
sinking clack and drop in currents of gravel.
          Instead of light there's air
getting higher and
oaks shedding themselves
                    into dark, thrown circles.

4.

          And here is where the trees have found themselves.
          Now the trunks lie flat: thin round tracks down a sandbank.
                They're making water by acting it
                trying to bring it about
                but getting closer and closer to being salted rock.
                Their bark rings off in trickles.

5.

The thing now
would be to haul
a scene of water through the range

because the dim comes on
first into valleys, up walls, while light's still stuck on the ceiling,
because its skin touches everything at once—
so that a cliff's no silhouette
but a single corner that turns,
and turns.

And naturally, the earth slides
  or, at least
        stars smear

        describing

        yellow lines
        of crusted powder.

Confidence

A stalk of light arrives
to grasp the roof's peak—

not a sigh from beneath, where a crowd
crosses the pale forum, snibbing purses.

The light folds itself up, a last ripple clears.

Angler's Reach

The lake's beaches are foothills, its islands thin tokens of earth.
They cannot convince me of substance.
I know that behind the lake

      snow strips ash and bullies sassafras
      into sallow drips. Still stands
make spurs of dormant tines. They spread their dead
through the creeks and under
      where gum pipes burnish, fuzz.

                Cloud furs the flood
                with grains and flocks.

      Even among that tendency toward boles
there are flats and strews: slight darkness marking like from like,
fused eventually to bright.   Rocks lose plaques.
                They lift inside years
                to slide past spangled heirs
           then clatter into catalogues of plates—

           clean but for the green cleaved there
           its dry hair muffling the ice.

How landed earth reforms itself as sunken bed, how fast it tracked
from being grass to weed, tree to hatching-hole.
The lake's come into the reach of sky

——

Its banks were never

are beyond return.

The hold

On the surface of the pool two lappers
                        have traced a diamond.

        It stretches as they rest, oblivious

to the nearby tree
where a web is pegged
from bough to grass
its nub falling flush
on a knot in the trunk.

The web swallows the breeze and swells

                    calipee, calipash,
            one of the swimmers
                crosses back

Autoptics

From just a few things, you get everything.
(Siri Hustvedt, *Mysteries of the Rectangle*)

Waitakere

Dull stolid   maybe blue black or
          impenetrable in parts:

streaming motorway   screwing
that mountain pass   a judgement

then a hyphen wavering over to Piha where clouds stop   start
                    waves   change

Titirangi

Break, glass, daughter.
              Kauri don't shade.

The roundabout chosen by a finger slanting from the sky—
visitors go into the light

streets bend tighter and tighter—
lining up wheels with poles.

Magnitude

That green and black could be unstretched canvas, lolling
16,000 yrs late   Shunt

open up it's edibly red   walled, see bone.

Kai iwi (1)

The lowest of the low
you've seen everything now

—tide and stack—the method for perfect drift—

and cracked it like a rib.

Kai iwi (2)

Soft throttle it, shudder to clay
and western radial trunks

gathered: megaflora bonfire never lit.

Well, that's it—veer away. How loose the fences are, how puny.

Cerulean

She plods off from the car, trailing a shadow—

her director left standing, shadowless
by the vehicle, seeing holes open up behind the girl—
still in focus, still darkly
against a desert's gaze.

I recall this feeling.

A resting place in that distant hill,
and the plodding, which grows
quieter as thoughts begin to talk.

Man Against a Background of Flames

Pen-point pushes shadow away,
draws it larger
to the surface of the page

as sun opens dunes
to stare at sand's dimensions.
Tipping every grain with dark.

It confirms a banksia dead. It makes knowledge——
the kind that catches on to everything it sees——
until the beach is soaked with uncertainty
and a poem with a poem's reason.

My vision dries, the page thickens and details,
feeding on brightness
with washes that crawl
one over the next
keeping what they touch
soft and unimpressed.
Their friction blanks the horizon——now a burning long shift of mood.

I write with one eye closed: a cloud narrows the world along fewer lines.
        It opens: words rush into its crisp canal
                like the blanketing glare before a storm
        presses light into space, flooding the world with too much sight.

                The horizon's grown
                I'm in its eye/x-rayed
                by clarity abundant
                and the unending glance of white.

The break

Bitter terns watch a woman's feet
kick against the dropping shore

her bluecapped head casting new waves
to the back of the ocean pool,
        reversing their lesson.

The terns pip and recede,
their notation muddled by a diver's motion
beyond the pool's walls—
splayed, he rides the mass ballooning—

as the swimmer's toes drill against a break
the blue cap bulging, centring
        velocity and its throat.

Re-mist

Young day, hang.
　　　　A cloud's in the garden, over
　　　　the bricked-up spring.
　　　　　　　　　　　Slip a limb down　　　easy.

Fingers before rain (the fog tightening headlights).

　　　　　　　Petrified and dull with wet. Crumpling, clutched.
Time let go——not into air, but the ground

to surface later——wheeling
faces, windows, coast.

*

Ticking down

Motion capture

Coming back over our patina
onto the east—silver lots,
the figure of coal.

The districts were silent
without insects, but home
we happen upon a dead rat

are satisfied with its hat of flies
and the sure set of teeth.

Lining space, drying time

From midway
up the bulge of sand, water turns
and carries stains of cloud, scrub.
The cormorant's shadow
barely moves but races
on the track of current—

a focused stripe of motion
running clear around
as the estuary plays its fast sheets
forward over rocks.
Time gliding across those dark tabs

and my ankle's quick
into the stripe. As I grow roots and barbs,
I see a bright fish coming down

dead instant orbit, distant
and headed to the black shore.

I claw the sand's crescent-shaped image
against the bend

its rocks wishing up sound:
the thought of it surfacing
on their tops white and bubbled,
cries and croaking humbles
that will begin sometime after I've stopped listening.

The fish and me aren't stones, we're acting out a shape.

       But the fish rounds the bend: I stay
               dropping steady into muck, waiting
               to hit a core of earth.

Morning has pulled noon and the whole creek
       through one grey glaze
already closing up where I've been.

The reader

Their books visible through front windows—
close to a ceiling, meeting one another.
On the street, someone's aftershave surrounds her like a city.

Every night she runs, lumbering with a dog

then breathes
from the pavement
trying to read their spines.

Bass & Flinders

for my parents

Blotting stars

a slug of cloud
        crosses the edge

and waves quake
slicked and rolling,
woken fixed on moonlight.
Gasp long and mute.

Whorls inscribed in the rock shelf.

A heron anchors
the big pool solid

and ignores two men noiselessly
headless, their toes upending white silt.

        Sound rises, the light comes on.

The Budawangs

Calving the mountains, seeing
a tight deck of blue planes,
you've begun to qualify their gaps
with distances kept in mind:
gullies from way back, measures of stock earth
impossibly stored within you
like the coast unseen yet guessed by Augustine.

But their tone's
incomprehensible. You return
two or three times a day.   Feel
their oily brushing—ti tree's reaching
rush and open fringe.

Before, you knew the way and why
light drops. Today something else
snags you: a ridge's edge, blunting
by the century, finishes with space not line. Never closing,
it feathers and dents
over and again making mountains
move.

It twinges with your projected touch.
Lets your eye cut filthy hubs of sandstone, too,
reach the ground gold rooms inside.

Touch it nowhere/belief

1.

      Black dusk
sifting birds
through the valley's vent. Blink—

where they've dissolved
tubes of shells mark the air.   That pink lime
working its fever, its moment of certainty

moment of doubt

blinking
from the ground

up turning

clear

2.

Only the old hutches sharpen in the foreground—

if I were fast as dust or dog
I'd miss them crumpled between the trunks,
but now I glimpse another:
that grave, uneven sketch
smarting from grass. The storm
runs through their wire
without a grip on hair or skin. I touch
the half-curve of a broken, cornered bowl
hatched by rasping shade.

The sharp wave
pulling up its curtain—

I can see through
far-off trembles

Pelagic

I don't yet feel but smell
       its body of ice & wing of air
       breath & rolled voices

then see the swollen face:
a screaming bole of fuel
ringing one note into its path.

     My fall brakes

          the crossing of forms below
          in the shallows.

Dead finish

In a few days the sea
   will have dried up

                        fine ruffled mangrove:
                        rusted ditch, reef guts.

Less the rolling
turbine aw
of coast's gentle, tidal wing—

                more
the red ping of stretching lugger bellies,
flutes of scale caving blue.

          More,
      foothills where grasses end—
         dead finish starts
             to print the rubble,
        singing granite dry.

        A few days further, hacks will grow into rockholes
                calling light
           which comes running out of a crook
grasping anything in reach (bough, culvert, whistling feather) turning
      them stiff.
The valley basin will stretch, weeping up beds of shatter
      cones and hairtail steps.

It has dreamt
of light and dream around the corner, when light and dream crumble
      against one constant, grainy edge. Their rushing ovoid,
      tracing that bowl of rock to tears:
                passage.

Koan

The plum
comes into the stone:
you are not a god.

Remember: forget
infinite faces.

You start to make up the news:
hammerhead astonishment, half-moon

and the art of sinking.

Happy, happy gaping
(it's so easy to guess the rest of history).

Notes

"Obit (Unmoved)"
Italicised phrase quotes Michael Dransfield's "Daylight rain"
(*Collected Poems,* ed. Rodney Hall, UQP, 1987).

"En abyme (Northland)"
Quotes from the original version of "The Islands", by Charles Brasch
(*Disputed Ground*, The Caxton Press, 1948).

"Touch it nowhere/belief"
The title is taken from Jennifer Maiden's poem, "The green storm"
(*Tactics*, UQP, 1974).

Acknowledgements

Versions of a number of these poems have appeared in *Ampersand, Five Poetry Journal, Mascara Literary Journal, Overland, PEN International Poetry Anthology* (Japan PEN Club, 2010), *Snorkel, The Salon Anthology: New Writing + Art 2005–2007* (eds. Bonny Cassidy & Katrina Schwarz, non-generic, 2007) and *Sun & Sleet: Poets Union Inc. Anthology* (Poets Union Inc, 2006).

Several of the poems were first published in a chapbook, *Said To Be Standing* (Vagabond Press, 2010), and in *Young Poets: An Australian Anthology* (ed. John Leonard, John Leonard Press, 2011).

I would like to acknowledge Asialink and the Malcolm Robertson Foundation for a 2008 literature fellowship spent in Japan where part of this collection was written.

My warmest thanks are due to Alan Wearne and Greg McLaren, who read an early manuscript, and to John Leonard and Andy Quan who provided invaluable editing of its final form. I must also thank the Sydney and Melbourne poetry workshops, which have not only helped to develop this work but have also provided the conversations, deprecation and trust that is so much needed by the solo work of poetry.

At the beginning and at the end of these poems, is Timothy Grey.

www.ingramcontent.com/pod-product-compliance
Lightning Source LLC
Chambersburg PA
CBHW031007090426
42737CB00008B/716